A TALE OF TWO SONS

Study Guide

JOHN MACARTHUR

THOMAS NELSON
Since 1798

NASHVILLE   DALLAS   MEXICO CITY   RIO DE JANEIRO   BEIJING

© 2008 by John MacArthur

The publishers are grateful to Terry Hadaway for his collaboration and writing skills in developing the content of this book.

All rights reserved. No portion of this book may be reproduced, stored in a retrieval system, or transmitted in any form or by any means—electronic, mechanical, photocopy, recording, scanning, or other—except for brief quotations in critical reviews or articles, without the prior written permission of the publisher.

Published in Nashville, Tennessee, by Thomas Nelson. Thomas Nelson is a registered trademark of Thomas Nelson, Inc.

Published in association with the literary agency of Wolgemuth & Associates, Inc.

Thomas Nelson, Inc. titles may be purchased in bulk for educational, business, fund-raising, or sales promotional use. For information, please e-mail SpecialMarkets@ThomasNelson.com.

All Scripture quotations in this book are from THE NEW KING JAMES VERSION. © 1982 by Thomas Nelson. Used by permission. All rights reserved.

ISBN 978-1-4185-2820-1

Printed in the United States of America

09 10 11 12 RRD 6 5 4 3

CONTENTS

❦ ONE ❧

Greatest Short Story. Ever.

"Jesus' intention in telling the story was not to impress His hearers with dramatic artistry. Rather, if we understand the parable correctly, its spiritual lessons leave a far more indelible impression on our hearts and minds than any literary analysis of the parable could accomplish."

—A Tale of Two Sons (p. 14)

Rewind

Many of the more familiar passages of Scripture are ripe with unnoticed theological truths that, if discovered and applied to our lives, could improve the quality of our relationships with God and each other. One such passage is the parable of the prodigal son.

Prodigal living is characterized by wasteful extravagance and wanton immorality (*MacArthur New Testament Commentary*, p. 220). The story of the Prodigal Son is more about the loving father than the wayward son and his spiteful brother. Jesus didn't tell the story in order to improve His reputation as a great storyteller; He told it to reveal some characteristics of God that had been veiled by the religious practices of the scribes and Pharisees. The cultural tension between Judaism and Jesus' ministry was underlying every word Jesus spoke.

Before we begin, we must remember that "the meaning of Scripture is not fluid. The truth of the Bible doesn't change with time or mean different things in different cultures. Whatever the text meant when it was originally

1

written, it still means today." Therefore, if we can grasp the original meaning of the parable, we can apply it to our lives today.

"It is all too easy to rip biblical stories out of their original contexts, force them into a postmodern frame of reference, and miss their full import."

1. Before beginning this study, what is your understanding of the meaning of the parable of the prodigal son?

2. We sometimes make the mistake of limiting our understanding of Scripture to what we read about Scripture. Read Mark 12:37b and identify the primary audience to whom Jesus spoke.

If this was Jesus' primary audience, what should be the degree of difficulty in determining the meanings of His words?

___ Only the religious elite can understand.

___ Only the avid Bible student can understand.

___ Only those who know the code can understand.

___ Most anyone can understand.

> "So if we expect to draw out of this parable what God wants us to learn and what He intended to reveal for our edification, we need to try to hear it the way Jesus' original audience heard it."

Rethink

The parable of the prodigal son was recorded by Luke, but not by the other gospel writers. Luke was the more detailed of the four gospel writers and was intimately familiar with Judaism and the stark contrast between traditional religion and Jesus' message.

3. Place the parable of the prodigal son on the timeline of Jesus' ministry by placing an X at the appropriate place.

| Baptism | Temptation | to Jerusalem | Arrest | Crucifixion | Resurrection |

4. Luke 9:51 says that Jesus "steadfastly set His face to go to Jerusalem." What is the significance of this statement?

> "In Old Testament times, scribes were those trained to record important events. By the time of the Babylonian exile, scribes were considered to be experts in the written Word of God. By New Testament times, scribes were a group of Pharisees with the responsibility of teaching, interpreting, and enforcing the Law of Moses." (*Holman Illustrated Bible Dictionary*, p. 1452)

5. The principle enemies of Jesus' ministry were the scribes and Pharisees. Based on your perception, what are some adjectives that can be used to describe the scribes and Pharisees?

What are the characteristics of modern-day scribes and Pharisees? In what settings might you encounter a modern scribe or Pharisee?

6. On page 10, it is said that the scribes and Pharisees "were *legalistic*—believing that the way to gain favor with God was by earning merit—and the best way to gain merit in God's eyes, they thought, was through fastidious observance of the law." Thus, they based their salvation on their own self-righteousness. As Christians, we know that our salvation is only based on the finished work of Christ. Yet we can sometimes allow forms of legalism and self-righteousness to creep into our own thinking. What are some ways in which we can become legalistic?

What are the effects of religious legalism in our lives?

7. The scribes and Pharisees "were also hypocritical . . . They valued the public display of religion more than private devotion and true righteousness." What are some ways in which this is evident in our society?

8. Jesus never entered into negotiations with the scribes and Pharisees; He stood His ground. Of course, this only heightened the tension. As a result, Jesus was at the top of their "Most Wanted" list. There have been times when we all have backed down rather than suffer the consequences of standing our ground on what we know to be right. In what areas of your life it is often easy to negotiate, or compromise, on our convictions?

What have been some of the consequences of your choosing to negotiate rather than stand for what you knew to be the truth?

9. Read Matthew 23:2–12. Jesus' words regarding the Pharisees should be seen in their context, but also applied across generations. When people begin to turn religion into their god, they inadvertently abandon the worship of the true God. Do your worship practices exalt God? If so, what are some things that direct your attention toward Him?

"Until we begin to comprehend the ideals and attitudes that shaped the culture, we can't expect to gain a full appreciation of the parable's main lesson."

Reflect

Tax collectors and gross sinners were the bane of society for the scribes and Pharisees. The very fact that Jesus associated with such undesirables was reason enough to seek to discredit Him and eventually kill Him. On more than one occasion, the Pharisees tried to back Jesus into a theological corner. But it is useless to debate theology with God and to refuse to humbly accept what He says is true. It was useless then; it remains useless today.

10. The scribes and Pharisees looked down their noses at two groups of people—the gross sinners and tax collectors. In that day, the religious elite distanced themselves from society's outcasts. In their world, the outcasts were notorious sinners and tax collectors. Who are the outcasts in our culture and how do you react when you encounter one of them?

11. Luke recorded three parables that explained Jesus' reasons for associating with society's outcasts. Keep in mind that parables were told for the purpose of illustrating one primary point. Read Luke 15:1–7. To reinforce his focus on the average person, Jesus told this story based on a flock of one hundred sheep. In that time, a flock of this size was average. What is the main point of the parable of the lost sheep?

12. Perhaps there were some in the crowd who were unfamiliar with the ways of a shepherd. For those people, Jesus offered a parable to which they could relate. Read Luke 15:8–10. A silver coin (a drachma) was equivalent in value to the Roman denarius, which was a day's wage for a Roman soldier. What is the main point of this parable?

React

This sets the stage for the parable of the prodigal son, sometimes referred to as the parable of the lost son. The Pharisees continued to question Jesus about His association with society's outcasts. This reflects their misunderstanding of what it meant to be a person of faith. The Pharisees saw the faith culture as exclusive; Jesus showed them that true faith and salvation is available to anyone, even the worst sinner, who will genuinely believe in Him.

13. Think about your church family and the ways in which you live out your Christian faith. How welcoming are you toward those who are different from you in personality, wealth, ethnicity, social status, cultural background, or physical appearance? On the line below, place an X indicating how willing you believe you are to accept those who are different from you.

very hesitant _____|_____ very willing
or exclusive   and welcoming

14. What are some ways in which your exclusiveness toward others sometimes surfaces?

What can you do to keep that from being a persistent problem?

Exclusiveness doesn't have to be intentional. We can inadvertently exclude people from our church family in a variety of ways. How "guest friendly" is your church campus? How do you respond to someone who isn't dressed like everyone else? How do you handle people who need special accommodations? Your answers to these questions will help you determine just how much like the Pharisees you are. You might be surprised. An honest evaluation of your present situation will set the tone for the remainder of this study.

15. Based on what you have learned in this study, what do you expect God to do in your life through the remainder of the study?

 ___ Nothing; I've already got this figured out.

 ___ I expect God to use me to change the lives of other people.

 ___ I might learn something, but I'm not as much in need as others I know.

 ___ I expect God to conform my thoughts to His thoughts.

16. As you pray, ask God to open your eyes and ears that you might see and hear His desire for you. As the study progresses, keep a journal detailing all of the ways in which God worked in and through this study.

A Wide-Angle Preview

Throughout Luke 15, Christ is describing and illustrating the celebratory joy
that fills heaven over the repentance of sinners.

— A Tale of Two Sons (p. 20)

Rewind

The effective study of the parable of the prodigal son begins with a basic understanding of the parable's primary purpose. As we progress through the study, we will have ample opportunity to dig deeper into the specifics of the characters and their actions. Before doing so, however, we must set in our minds the basic meaning of the parable.

Everything we need to know about the parable is contained in the parable itself. There are other passages of Scripture that help us understand the context in which the parable was set, but they are not required for a thorough understanding. The Pharisees were disturbed that Jesus socialized with people they despised—the tax collectors and sinners. The Pharisees operated from the belief that godliness was primarily a matter of external appearances. Naturally, their views produced exclusiveness.

"To borrow the Pharisees' own words (without the sinister slant they put on it), Jesus was *truly* 'a friend of tax collectors and sinners!' (Luke 7:34)."

1. What are some other situations in which Jesus associated with society's so-called undesirable people?

What was Jesus' reason for spending time with such people?

2. Jesus didn't simply fit the spiritually needy people into His otherwise busy schedule; He sought them out and planned to spend time with them. What are the personal challenges you must overcome in order to be used by God in this way?

"He was a true friend of sinners—the most authentic kind of friend. He served them and reached out to them and laid hold of their lives."

Rethink

The redemptive theme of Jesus' ministry is foundational to the narrative in Luke 15. At no point in His ministry did Jesus ever compromise His holiness. He maintained His purity in spite of the sinfulness of those to whom He ministered. His purpose was not to condone sin. Rather, He released people from the bondage of sin and set them on the path of salvation and true righteousness.

In reaching out to society's downtrodden and outcasts, Jesus was accused of consorting with sinners. This was reason enough for the Pharisees to discredit His ministry. However, it is important to note that Jesus did not approve of the sins of those to whom He ministered.

3. What practical steps can you take to reach out to the spiritually needy people in your life (such as unsaved family members, friends, neighbors, and co-workers)?

4. Put yourself in the place of the Pharisees. How do you think you would have responded to Jesus' relationship with society's outcasts?

___ I would have encouraged Him in His ministry.

___ I would have thought poorly of Him.

"Jesus was accused of violating the Sabbath (Luke 6:2). Judaism banned thirty-nine tasks on the Sabbath. Most of them were categorized as "work," such as tying a knot. Jesus observed the Sabbath as a day of worship, but He did not choose to obey the legalistic restrictions that had been attached to the Sabbath. This was one source of conflict between Jesus and the Pharisees." (*Holman Illustrated Bible Dictionary*, p. 1426)

5. Why do you think so many self-admitted sinners became disciples of Jesus? Why do you think the self-righteous Pharisees resisted His message of salvation?

How should Jesus' example of ministering to those who were spiritually in need (regardless of their social status) affect our ministries to others?

6. Throughout His ministry, many tax collectors and sinners were drawn to Jesus and His teaching. What circumstances did God use to draw you to Jesus (cf. John 6:44)?

What does God use to draw people to Jesus today?

7. The scribes and Pharisees worked hard to convince people not to follow Jesus. Many people listened because they had been taught to respect and honor the scribes and Pharisees. What societal "authorities" today compete with the Holy Spirit for attention (examples: false religion, secular media, Christian traditionalism)? How should we respond to such "authorities" (cf. 2 Corinthians 10:3–6)?

8. The more Jesus dealt with difficult subjects and challenging themes, the more people were persuaded to join in the opposition to His ministry. What is your response when God's Word "steps on your toes"?

___ I agree with God's Word.

___ I justify my attitude or actions as acceptable.

___ I seek out a less restrictive interpretation of the passage.

___ I assume the instructions were intended for a different time or culture.

___ Other: _____

What have been some of the consequences of your responses identified above?

9. As long as Jesus was feeding His followers and performing miracles, people followed. But when Jesus began challenging their ways of life and their religious hypocrisy, they quickly turned away. Read Luke 14:26–35. How do these words affect you?

___ They weren't spoken to me.

___ They are strong, but have little effect on me.

___ They are a message for me today.

___ This is a part of the Bible we shouldn't really focus on.

"Within six months, some of the very same common people who once 'heard Him gladly' (Mark 12:37) would be screaming for His blood."

Reflect

The parables in Luke 15 all make the same point. The first two are much shorter than the parable of the prodigal son, but they deserve some investigation. The prime targets of these parables were the scribes and Pharisees. Though Jesus never attacked them, He did attack their hypocrisy and wickedness.

10. Read Luke 15:1–7. List the characteristics of sheep.

What was the primary responsibility of a shepherd?

Why is the image of sheep and a shepherd so relevant to the way in which God deals with us? What does the shepherd's response to finding the sheep reveal about God's response to finding someone who is lost?

"So here's a perfect picture of divine grace: the shepherd in this short parable does *all* the work. He seeks and finds the lost lamb, and then he carries it home on his shoulders."

11. One of the earliest symbols of Christianity was the shepherd carrying the sheep home. Read Isaiah 40:11 and compare the image in that passage to the image presented in this parable.

In the parable, the shepherd did all the work. In real life, Jesus Christ did the work by dying on the cross for us. Why do so many people still believe that their salvation is based on what they do rather than what Jesus did?

React

Jesus' second parable teaches the same lesson. This one, however, deals with a lost coin and a woman's desperate search for it. As in the story of the sheep, the woman lost a portion of what she had. But because she lost something valuable, she searched for it.

12. Read Luke 15:8–10, paying attention to the reaction of the woman to finding the lost coin. What does her reaction reveal about God's reaction to a person's salvation?

13. If a person's salvation brings joy to God, how should that reality motivate our desire to share the good news of His love and salvation with those who don't know Him?

Jesus often used parables to keep truths from being understood by unbelievers (see Luke 8:10), but that wasn't His purpose in these parables. Jesus wanted to teach the Pharisees something about themselves that they could not see or refused to see.

14. Review the two earlier parables and identify each of the following:

Luke 15:1–7   Luke 15:8–10

Something lost and found:

The role of the seeker:

The reaction after the recovery:

15. The parable of the prodigal son presents some additional roles within the same basic theme. Read the information on pages 33–35 and match the role with the element or person in the parable.

  __ The younger brother   A. God

  __ The father   B. The Pharisees

  __ The older brother   C. The person who is lost

16. As we move into a deeper study of this parable, carefully evaluate your life as it relates to these parables. Which statement below best represents you?

  __ I am like the lost sheep, lost coin, and Prodigal Son. I need God to find me.

___ I am like the shepherd, the woman, and the father—
seeking the lost so that they can be brought into a right
relationship with God.

___ I am like the older brother—out of harmony with
heaven's joy.

⁍ THREE ⁌

His Shameless Demand

As the parable begins, the younger son appears to be cast in the scoundrel's role as the central character.

— A Tale of Two Sons (p. 41)

Rewind

We are familiar with stories in which there are villains and heroes. The parable of the prodigal son is one such story, but the roles played by the main characters are varied. Each character is deserving of careful consideration. We begin with the younger son—the scoundrel in the early going. (Later, we'll see the older brother is portrayed as the scoundrel.)

This parable supports the overall theme of Luke 15—heaven's joy over a sinner who repents. The younger son represents the sinner who repents, the father demonstrates the joy of heaven, and the older son represents the attitude of the Pharisees. Though set in the first century, the lessons of this parable are relevant today.

"The young man is a classic illustration of an undisciplined young person who wastes the best part of his life through extravagant self-indulgence and becomes a slave to his own lust and sin."

1. Which do you think best describes *prodigal?*

___ Youthful rebellion

___ A wayward son or daughter

___ Reckless wastefulness

___ Irresponsible behavior

Other than this story, when have you heard the word *prodigal* used?

___ Daily in reference to _____

___ Occasionally

___ Never

2. The younger brother is a living picture of the effects of sin in a person's life. Why do you think so many people find this kind of life so attractive?

"The young man's request, as Jesus described it, was outrageous, impudent, and grossly dishonoring to the father."

Rethink

The young man was not yet married and had a lack of respect for his father. He preferred sowing his wild oats to working alongside his brother on the family farm. His actions were totally self-centered and contrary to the way in which sons treated their fathers and their inheritances.

The passing of the inheritance to the children was normally handled in accordance with traditions that had been handed down for generations. The *law of primogeniture* awarded a double share of the inheritance to the oldest son. There was a stipulation that allowed for the awarding of the double portion to the youngest son, but that was a rare occurrence. The problem with the younger son related more to his uncaring attitude toward his family tradition. Some might even question the young man's affection for his father. The younger man was only interested in immediate gratification.

3. Consider your life as it compares to the young man in the parable. In what areas of life do you seek immediate gratification?

4. What does the desire for immediate gratification say about a person's attitude toward other aspects of her or her life?

"Once disowned by a father, there was almost no way for a rebellious child to come back and regain his position in the family. If wanted back at all, he must make restitution for whatever dishonor he caused the family and for whatever possessions he might have taken when he ran away. Even then, he might expect to forfeit many of the rights that he previously enjoyed as a family member. He could certainly forget about receiving any further inheritance."

5. The young man deserved nothing from his father. How would you respond if someone treated you the way the son treated his father?

How should God respond to us when we treat Him similarly?

6. On page 49, the young man wanted to be rid of every obligation, to cast off all restraint, and to remove himself from his father's authority. He wanted to run. What would cause a person to run from God?

How does God respond to those who choose to run from Him?

7. Even if a father chose to award an inheritance to his sons before he died, the sons were required by the *Mishnah* to hold their inheritance until the death of their father. In other words, the father maintained ownership until his death. The younger son's taking of the inheritance and subsequent squandering of the inheritance was more serious than we realize. Review the actions of the son and list all of the bad choices he made.

8. The Prodigal was primarily interested in getting out of the family so he could live the way he wanted. He had little interest in living according to the laws of society or the expectations of his family. What might have been the young man's reasons for wanting to get away from his family?

   What do the young man's actions illustrate about the heart of sinful people?

9. Put yourself in the father's position. What might have been some of the emotions you would have encountered as your son turned on you?

How would the certain public embarrassment have affected your response to your son?

"Any self-respecting father in that culture would naturally feel he *had* to disgrace the son as publicly as possible— giving him the ceremonial slap across the face, a public denunciation, formal dismissal from the family, and possibly even a funeral."

Reflect

The father's response to his son was surprising. In verse 12 we see that the father gave the younger son what he wanted. The father granted the disrespectful wish of the insolent young man. This would have sparked a reaction from the legalists listening to Jesus' story.

10. "Livelihood" is a translation of the Greek word *bios*, which means "life." Some translations use the word *property* in this verse. Reread verse 12 with the idea of "life" in mind. What did the father really give his son?

What does the father's response teach about God's attitude toward us?

"The Prodigal took his portion of the family wealth without looking back. He had exactly what he wanted: absolute freedom."

11. The father's actions reveal that he was truly loving; he wasn't a tyrant. He was willing to be humiliated publicly rather than destroy the relationship between him and his son. He had offered his love to his son, but his love was rejected.

How does God respond when we reject His love?

React

Jesus' story was about His love for sinners. The father's love for his son represents God's love for rebellious humanity. God would be justified to turn His back on anyone who rejects Him, but He chooses to love us with persistence and patience.

12. In what ways have you experienced God's . . .

mercy?

lovingkindness?

goodwill?

longsuffering?

13. Why do you think God allows people to rebel against Him?

14. Review Luke 15:11–31 and create a short profile of the younger son. What were the strong points of his character? What were his weaknesses?

15. How did your life before Christ reflect the attitudes of the younger son?

In what ways are you sometimes still like the younger son?

In what ways are you different from the younger son?

What shameless demands have you made of your heavenly Father?

Why did you make those demands? What was your ultimate goal when making the demands?

❊ FOUR ❊

His Shameful Misconduct

This part of the story culminates in the absolute meltdown of the Prodigal's life.
His own lusts prove uncontrollable. He finds himself enslaved in a horrific bondage from
which he is powerless to free himself.

— A Tale of Two Sons (p. 55)

Rewind

The younger son's attitude led him to mistreat his father, and the trouble wasn't over for the young man—things were about to go from bad to worse. Leaving his father's home wouldn't solve the problem. The freedom he sought would be his downfall. Separated from his father's authority, the younger son was quickly enslaved to his own selfish desires and sinful nature.

Like many people today, the younger son's freedom became his bondage. He started down a path that ultimately landed him in appalling circumstances. He traded a stable home life for homelessness. He traded his father's table for a share of the pig's food.

> "This young man was fed up with all his responsibilities, tired of being accountable to his father, and sick of every relationship in his life—especially with his father and older brother. Now that he finally had the means, he could hardly wait to make his escape."

1. Read Luke 15:13. What does the phrase "gathered all together" mean?

   __ Liquidated his possessions

   __ Packed his bags

   __ Sorted the family treasures, taking what was his

   __ Had a garage sale

   Describe a time when you have wanted to run away. What was the cause? What were the results?

2. In desperation, the younger son had to accept far less than market value for his possessions. Why was this so?

   What does his eagerness to liquidate his portion of the property say about his desire to run away?

"That perfectly illustrates the foolishness of the sinner. He wants to get away from God, and he is more concerned with doing it *now* than he is with what it might cost him in the future."

Rethink

The young man did more than run to a neighboring village. Scripture tells us that he "journeyed to a far country." This meant that he abandoned his family, his culture, and his faith.

In comparison to the young man, we might see ourselves as having never given into the temptation to embrace prodigal living. Yet many people who know the joy of their salvation squander it in selfish living. It is easy to take God's gifts and then use them for personal gain. It is easy to make pleasing self more important than pleasing God. These are examples of modern prodigal living.

3. Many hearing Jesus' story might have rebutted with claims that they never had run away from home or abandoned their families. But Jesus' comments apply to more than the physical act of running away. What are some modern situations to which this parable speaks?

4. Why would someone run from family, God, and authority? What is the end result of running from God?

"It was unthinkable that any Jewish young person would journey by choice into Gentile lands and willingly take up permanent residence there (or worse, become a vagrant so far from home) in order to indulge in licentious living."

5. Upon review, how severe was the young man's . . . (place an X on each line)

	MILD	MEDIUM	EXTREME
materialism?	|————————|————————|
greed?	|————————|————————|
foolishness?	|————————|————————|

Now go back and place an O representing yourself in each area.

How do you measure up against the younger son?

___ I'm a modern-day prodigal.

___ I'm not a prodigal yet, but I'm headed there.

___ I'm definitely better than the Prodigal Son.

___ I can't relate to the Prodigal Son at all.

6. In running to a Gentile land, the young man exhibits total disdain for everything he had ever been. Why would the Pharisees and scribes think that the younger brother was the villain?

7. People who are self-righteous are generally harder on people like the younger son. That's the way it was with the scribes and Pharisees. The Pharisees considered every aspect of Gentile culture to be unclean. Therefore, even associating with Gentiles

was a transgression. The Pharisees would have been glad to get rid of such a despicable character. How do you respond to the "despicable characters" in your life?

8. What do you think was going through the mind of the older brother? Why didn't he step in and defend his father?

9. The actions of the younger brother show a lack of love for his father. What is revealed by the older brother's lack of response to the situation?

___ He loved his father more.

___ He was an innocent bystander.

___ He didn't really love his father either.

___ He was glad to get rid of his little brother.

"Although the father was a loving, generous, kindly man who provided abundant gifts for his two sons, both of his sons cared more for the father's wealth than they did for the father himself."

Reflect

The younger son took off for a life that maybe he had heard about from others. It was the place where all of today's problems disappear and a new reality is born.

10. What was the primary focus of the younger son?

__ To make a good living

__ To get an education

__ To be a good role model

__ To have fun

What might someone with this desire do today?

"He squandered a fortune in no time, spending his inheritance in the pursuit of wickedness. The elder brother later summed up the Prodigal's lifestyle in these words: he 'devoured [his father's] livelihood with harlots' (v. 30)."

11. Read Galatians 6:7–8. What is the biblical response to a desire for pleasure above responsibility?

React

Sin *never* delivers what it promises, and the pleasurable life sinners think they are pursuing *always* turns out to be precisely the opposite: a hard road that leads inevitably leads to ruin and the ultimate, literal dead-end.

12. What do the following Scripture passages say about sin?

Romans 6:23

Romans 8:13

James 1:15

13. The young man initially seemed to get what he desired. But as his money evaporated, so did his "friends" and popularity. What is the real connection between self-gratification and real peace?

The younger brother was left with nothing. His money was gone. His friends were gone. He was in a strange country and had nothing. He got what he asked for and the results were his fault.

14. Life turned quickly for the Prodigal. His brief lavish lifestyle was replaced by severe need and hunger. You might never have experienced severe hunger. What is the worst personal disaster you have experienced?

15. Read the description of the European famine during the medieval period (page 66) in *A Tale of Two Sons*. How does this description make you feel?

16. What would you say to someone who was pursuing this lifestyle?

17. In what ways have you been a prodigal? What has been the cost of your choices? Is there an area of your life right now in which you are rebelling against something you know God wants you to do?

Pray, asking God to restore you to a right relationship with Him and all those around you. Confess your sin and seek to please Him with your life.

❧ F I V E ❧

His Turning Point

*Some people are so determined to have their own way that
even when they are being force-fed the distasteful consequences
of their transgressions, they still will not give up the pursuit.*

— A Tale of Two Sons (p. 70)

Rewind

The young man began his journey to the far land with expectations of self-indulgence and personal pleasure. Instead, he discovered bondage and sorrow. Beneath this experience was a principle that was as old as creation—we will never find true peace and joy through doing things our way!

The Prodigal inadvertently headed down a dead-end road. By the time he realized what was happening, it was too late. He had to deal with some things he never anticipated. He had no friends or family members. His money was exhausted. He had no source of income and he was hungry. Certainly he had flashbacks to the days in his father's home when he had every need met. The very thing he sought to escape soon became a reminder of what could have been if he had stayed home.

"One thing is certain: if the Prodigal had known it would come to this, he never would have set out on his quest."

1. Read Luke 15:17. What does the phrase "when he came to himself" mean?

   __ "When he realized he had no other options"

   __ "When he thought through his situation from a truthful perspective"

   __ "When he had run out of people to take advice from"

   __ "When his luck ran out"

   Describe a time when you have been in a situation similar to that of the young man.

   What brought you to your senses?

2. Page 70 in A *Tale of Two Sons* says, "I have known people whose lives were totally laid waste by the fallout of some favorite sin. They might be literally sick to death of their sin's repercussions, and yet they will not give up the sin itself." Do you know people who fit this description?

   __ Yes

   __ No

Has this description ever been true of you? If so, how was it resolved? If not, how have you protected yourself from this temptation?

"Going home . . . would mean accepting responsibility, living under accountability, and submitting to authority—all of which he had fled in the first place."

Rethink

The Prodigal wanted to avoid owning up to his bad decision, so he went to work for a farmer. His job was feeding pigs. Feeding animals wasn't a bad thing, but the Jews weren't fond of pigs. Jesus' inclusion of this detail would have demonstrated to the scribes and Pharisees just how desperate the young man was.

People do strange things in desperate times. It would have made sense for the young man to seek out his father and make things right, but desperation and pride interfered with his ability to do the right thing.

3. Read Luke 15:13–16. If you had been in the same situation as the Prodigal Son, how do you think you would have responded and why?

4. The young man wouldn't return to his father because of pride and stubbornness. How do pride and stubbornness affect your life?

"In other words, the Prodigal's desperation had already reached such a critical point that he literally became a beggar. By now he was probably filthy, unkempt, reduced to extreme poverty, and all he could do was beg."

5. The Prodigal didn't look for a job; he became a beggar. The image is that of the young man refusing to take no for an answer. He begged for help and wouldn't go away. He was given the most demeaning job imaginable. What would be the most demeaning job in your community? Why do you think people take that kind of job? How do you feel about people who perform that job?

6. The job offer for the Prodigal was more of an insult than an opportunity since the scribes and Pharisees viewed anything to do with pigs as being highly immoral and offensive. In order to perform the job, the Prodigal had to live with the pigs. This would have been a very harsh, isolated, rocky area that was good for nothing else. The young man wasn't living in a farmhouse. Rethink the story to this point. What offenses against his father and his faith had the Prodigal committed?

On a scale of 1 to 10, with 1 being no compassion and 10 being outrageous compassion, what level of compassion do you think the scribes and Pharisees had for the young man?

7. The young man reached his lowest point when he started looking hungrily at the feed that was being provided to the pigs. This was the most extreme form of desperation. Thinking about your life, what has been your most desperate experience? What did you learn about God in that experience?

8. Humans could not easily digest the scraps fed to the pigs. But the young man was so needy that his judgment was compromised. In what areas of life is your judgment severely affected by your needs?

When you find yourself in one of these situations, what is your most likely response?

__ Woe is me! (Anxiety or depression)

__ I'm a victim! (Shifting blame)

__ This can't be happening! (Denial)

__ I need help from God. (Dependence)

9. The carob pods were an emergency food supply for pigs and cattle. For the livestock, they represented hope in the midst of famine. What do you tend to rely on in the midst of difficult circumstances?

___ My financial resources

___ My social status

___ My ingenuity

___ My relationship with God

Are you pleased with your initial response to this question? If not, what do you need to do to change your response?

"In the Pharisees' estimation, [the Prodigal] had essentially *become* one of the pigs. The only way he could get any lower was to be cast into the pit of hell—which, as far as they were concerned, was practically unavoidable for him now and a punishment well deserved."

Reflect

As Jesus told this parable, He described the Prodigal in terms that would have made the rebellious son totally reprehensible. To the scribes and Pharisees, the young man was beyond hope and irredeemable.

10. The "hopeless" in our society often are viewed from a perspective similar to that of the scribes and Pharisees. The religious rulers had no compassion; they had only spite for the young man. He made choices that had terrible consequences. When you see someone who has made similar mistakes, what is your attitude? (Place an X on the line below.)

contempt ——————————— | ——————————— compassion

We all have made rebellious choices (sin) that have separated us from God. When you were detestable to God, what was His attitude? (Place an O on the line above representing God's level of compassion toward us.) Why is it so easy for us to hold attitudes that are inconsistent with God's attitude?

"Our sin is a calculated, deliberate violation of the relationship we have with our Creator."

11. Describe your present relationship with God in terms of . . .

a. The quality and quantity of the time spent in devotion to Him:

b. Your desire to please God with every aspect of your life:

c. Your desire to give God your best:

12. Based on your descriptions above, does your relationship with God need improvement? Why or why not?

React

Our sin is the ultimate show of disrespect to a loving Father. Even the most insignificant sin is a serious offense to our holy God, and it can also have serious consequences. Sin never produces good fruit; only bad.

13. Read Ephesians 2:12. How would you describe the existence of an unredeemed person?

14. The evil motives that guided the Prodigal are comparable to the evil motives that guide us. Read Romans 8:7–8. Rewrite this passage below in your own words.

In reality, we all are prodigal sons and daughters. We are guilty of the same things that landed the young man in a foreign land without food and without hope.

15. When you think about your actions today, what do you think was your primary motivation?

    __ Discovering God's goodness

    __ Pursuing self-gratification

    Notice that there are only two choices, and one of them will be true of your motivations today. Rethink the question and explain your reasons for living this way.

16. The ultimate destination of a life of unrestrained sin is spiritual bankruptcy, emptiness, destitution, and loneliness. Yet, some people believe they will be able to live according to their agendas without suffering the consequences. Describe a decision you have made in which you chose to pursue God's ways rather than the world's ways.

17. The Prodigal was forced to see himself for who he really was. He was in need of salvation from his terrible existence. He decided that he needed to go home. Was there ever a time in your life when you found yourself in similar circumstances? What happened?

Pray, asking God to give you a desire to live each day in the shelter of your Father's home, trusting Him for your provisions and honoring Him with your thoughts and actions.

His Return

For the scribes and Pharisees, the notion that someone like the Prodigal Son could ever find any kind of forgiveness or redemption was far beyond their comprehension.

— A Tale of Two Sons (p. 85)

Rewind

The scribes and Pharisees saw righteousness as the result of one's adherence to a religious system that had been overcomplicated with legalistic inter-pretations and human requirements. Once someone broke the rules to the extent that the Prodigal had, righteousness was a virtual impossibility.

Though the Pharisees liked themselves, they despised others. They eas-ily justified their prejudices and defended their judgments. To them, the logical conclusion of Jesus' story was the pitiful state of the young man with the pigs. The last thing they wanted was for the story to end with the Prodigal's repentance.

"He confessed freely that he was not worthy of any more grace or favor."

1. The Prodigal had to come to the point of acknowledging his sin. Rather than look at life from his perspective, he had to look at life from God's perspective. What do you think was the primary obstacle to the Prodigal's repentance?

Is that obstacle still a problem for people today? Why or why not?

2. Read Luke 15:17–19. While in the foreign land, the young man had encountered people whom the Jews despised. In his desire to seek reconciliation with his father, the Prodigal revealed that he understood the twofold nature of his sin. In what two ways did the young man sin?

How do we sin in these ways today?

"Rather than trying to evade responsibility for his sin, the younger son would face it squarely. Rather than running further away, he would go home. He would make a full confession and throw himself on his father's mercy."

Rethink

The Prodigal knew that he had forfeited his right to sonship in his father's household. But he also acknowledged that the life of a servant in his father's house was far better than the life of a pig feeder in a foreign land.

The young man decided that he had experienced the worst shame there was. From this point forward, nothing could be as bad as what he was doing. The very thing he fled became the very thing he needed most.

3. The Prodigal had to make an honest evaluation of his situation. What had he done?

What have you done?

4. The image of God in the role of the father in the story comes breaking through. The Prodigal knew where to turn for help. He simply needed the courage and humility to do what was needed. When you run into difficulties, how do you attempt to solve them? Order the following sources of help from 1 to 5, depending on how you think you attempt to solve your problems.

___ Seek help from a friend

___ Seek help from a family member

___ Seek help from a book or other source

___ Seek help from God

___ Solve the problem myself

Based on your understanding of the Bible, what should be your first action?

> "He knew he did not deserve even a hired servant's status in his father's household, but he also knew his father to be generous, and that got him thinking."

5. The Prodigal had thought of no one other than himself. Now, however, his thoughts turned to his father. Based on what the young man had done, what were some of the ways the father could have treated him?

6. Read Romans 6:16 and explain the condition of an unrepentant sinner.

When the young man remembered his father, did he remember his kindness and mercy or his rage and condemnation? Why?

The Prodigal knew his father's character. He understood that a person's character guides his or her actions. He was optimistic about returning to his father because he knew what kind of person his father was.

When you think about God, you should consider His character. You know His track record and how He has acted in the past. You know He is consistent in all His ways and that God's ways are right. Why, then, do so many people refuse to seek God's mercy?

7. The young man would soon die if he did not do something to change his situation. He stopped thinking about his wants and considered his needs. How do you know the difference between your needs and wants?

8. True repentance often begins with an accurate assessment of one's own condition. How would you describe the Prodigal's condition?

How would you describe your condition?

The Pharisees refused to recognize their true condition. What prevents people from being honest about their spiritual condition?

9. Reconsider the Prodigal's social descent from his original home to his pig-feeding days. When he lived at home, what might have been the young man's attitude toward his father's servants?

How did that attitude change? What caused it to change?

"The Greek word translated 'hired servants' in this verse is *misthios*. It refers to day laborers—the lowest of all workers on the economic scale. In the first-century culture, that kind of hired servant held a much lower status than a slave."

Reflect

There was a difference between slaves and hired servants. The hired servants were lower on the social scale than were slaves. Some slaves actually managed certain aspects of the family business. The hired servants or day laborers had no master. They were mostly unskilled and homeless.

10. The Prodigal had fallen from a life of relative luxury to being the poorest of the poor. Where once he had everything, he now had nothing. Hired servants had little hope except for a provision in Leviticus 19:13 that guaranteed them daily payment for the work done. But even that wasn't enough to live on. He remembered his father's generosity. What characteristics of God do you remember most often?

"The Greek word for 'repentance' throughout the New Testament is *metanoia*, and its literal meaning speaks of a change of mind—a reversal in one's thinking."

11. Repentance is more than you changing your opinion about God. It is a radically new way of seeing life—a new worldview. Read Ezekiel 11:19–20 and describe the concept of repentance from this viewpoint.

12. The Prodigal's brokenness prepared him for repentance. Describe your repentance experience. Was it preceded by brokenness? If so, describe that situation.

React

True brokenness turns the fleeing sinner into the seeking sinner. It is one thing to regret one's actions; it's another to be truly broken. Regret has more to do with being sorry for being found out. Brokenness is one's response to the realization that God's heart has been broken.

13. What is the difference between regret and brokenness?

14. Repentance leads one to seek mercy. Describe your experience with repentance. At what point did you discover your need for repentance? What was the subsequent effect of your repentance?

15. Read Ezra 9:6 and Luke 9:23. What was Ezra's cry? What was Jesus' response?

16. The Prodigal realized his need to repent and return to his father. His concern was how to go about doing it. What are some things people do in response to their need for repentance?

17. Read Luke 15:20. This was repentance in action. The Prodigal Son had wronged his father so he needed to confess to his father. His other option was to feel sorry for himself. Compare the attitude of the young man when he left his father's home and when he returned. How had he changed?

Pray, asking God to give you a desire to live in humble submission to God and His desires. If there are areas of unconfessed sin in your life, ask Him to break your heart so that you will truly seek repentance.

SEVEN

His Forgiveness

*The scribes and Pharisees surely expected the Prodigal Son's father
to drop the hammer hard on the wayward youth.*

— A Tale of Two Sons (p. 105)

Rewind

Any self-respecting father would do everything he could to protect his family name. The embarrassment caused by the younger son was enough to warrant a harsh response to the son's return.

We must continue to keep in mind that Jesus told the parable in terms that were familiar to the scribes and Pharisees. In the same situation, the Jewish leaders knew exactly what they would have done. They were skeptical about the Prodigal's repentant return home and they probably anticipated a very unforgiving response from the father.

"No matter where [the Prodigal Son] went and what he did after that, he would be hopelessly defiled in the Pharisee's estimation."

1. We know what the Prodigal Son did to defile himself, but what about us? What are the things we do that break God's heart?

   Why are we so reluctant to seek forgiveness for the things we do that break His heart?

2. The Pharisees weren't opposed to forgiveness; they did oppose instant and total forgiveness. They believed the young man needed to earn forgiveness over time. How does this philosophy affect our understanding of forgiveness?

"Not only could he never be a son again, but he would have no status at all. Why should he? *He* was the one who had renounced his own heritage and chose to live like a Gentile."

Rethink

The Prodigal Son had to wonder how his father would respond, since he knew he was utterly unworthy of his father's compassion and mercy. The Pharisees would have likewise seen him as undeserving of forgiveness. You might be thinking the same thing.

3. The Bible teaches that we are utterly unworthy of God's forgiveness. Why is that?

   How can God be righteous and yet forgive sinners? How does Christ's sacrifice on the cross make our forgiveness possible?

   How quickly does God forgive? How complete is His forgiveness?

   Read Psalm 103:12. God said that He puts away our sins as far as the east is from the west. Why did God use east and west rather than north and south?

4. The Pharisees viewed the young man's situation in a way that is comparable to a modern-day parole. If he maintained his innocence for a period of time, he could shuck off some of the baggage associated with his misbehavior. Forgiveness was a progression that took time. If this had been the attitude of the father, how might he have responded to his son's return?

"So what happened next was a seismic jolt to the Pharisees' worldview. Their eyes would roll and their heads would shake with shock and outrage at the reception the father gave the Prodigal Son."

5. The Prodigal desperately needed his father's resources. In what ways do we desperately need the resources of our heavenly Father?

6. Read Luke 15:18–19. What was the young man anticipating?

The father was within his rights to make a public spectacle of the young man. In doing so, the father would reassert his position of authority and control. The best the young man could hope for was a nonhostile encounter with his estranged father. What modern situations could be similar to this situation?

7. Whereas the young man once rebelled against his father's authority, he now was on a collision course with that same authority. He had no way of knowing how he would be received. All he knew was how he deserved to be treated. Based on our sin, how do we deserve to be treated by God?

What keeps Him from treating us this way?

8. The Prodigal left home as a son and returned as a potential employee. The father had the right to spell out the details of the employment arrangement and any privileges the son might enjoy. In other words, the young man was completely at the mercy of his father. In what ways does this represent the act of redemption and the salvation experience?

9. Read Genesis 50:15–21. Joseph had every reason to punish his brothers for all they had done to him, but he showed mercy. Joseph was a picture of mercy in action. Most Jewish people knew the story of Joseph, but no one expected that kind of mercy to be shown to the rebellious son. What does the story of Joseph teach about God's love and mercy?

"No one would expect anything like that from the Prodigal's father—not the Prodigal Son himself, not the villagers in his father's community, not his elder brother, not the people in Jesus' audience, and certainly not the Pharisees."

Reflect
"When he was still a great way off, his father saw him and had compassion, and ran and fell on his neck and kissed him" (Luke 15:20).

10. Could it be that the father was looking for his son's return? His reaction confirms that assumption. Read verse 20. What in that verse indicates that the father anticipated his son's homecoming?

"Obviously, the heartache had not yet worn off, because the father was still watching. And he kept watching daily, heartbroken but hopeful, privately bearing the unspeakable pain of suffering love for his son."

11. Can you visualize the father sitting on his rooftop scanning the horizon anxiously awaiting the day when his wayward son would return? What does this image teach about God's attitude toward us?

12. The village was busy with merchants and conversation. Word of the son's return probably spread as quickly as did the word of his departure. The father had long known how he would respond. His only concern was the "if." How does God plan to respond when a wayward sinner returns to Him?

13. Read Romans 8:30. How does this verse describe God's redemptive work?

React

The father might have run to meet his son before his son was met with the scorn of the villagers. Their response to the son was in line with that of the scribes and Pharisees. Had they reached the young man before his father did, they might have discouraged his return.

14. The Bible says that the father ran to his son. What is the significance of his running?

How did the Pharisees view the father's act of humility?

15. The father embraced his son and kissed him. He was overjoyed at the return of his rebellious son. How does God react when we humbly return to Him?

How does repentance relate to the image provided by this scene?

16. Take another look at Luke 15:21. The son began expressing his repentance only to have the father initiate a banquet celebrating his return. What was more important—the words the son said or the condition of his heart?

Many times, we get focused on the technicalities of what we want to say to God—the external. Yet God is more interested in the condition of our hearts—the internal. What are three things you can do to focus on internal heart change rather than merely external (behavior) change?

1.

2.

3.

17. The Bible teaches that sin has a price that must be paid. The payment is never in the things we do or the rituals we keep. The biblical idea is that of substitutionary atonement—that Jesus Christ died in the place of those who believe in Him, paying the punishment that they deserved. Describe the importance of His substitutionary atonement to you.

Pray, asking God to constantly remind you of His grace and love. As a result, ask Him to empower you to show that grace and love to those who have yet to experience it.

{ E I G H T }

His Generosity

The servants must have watched in amazement as their master reached his son, embraced him (stinking, pig-slop-stained rags and all), and started kissing him as if the boy were a returning hero.

— A Tale of Two Sons (p. 125)

Rewind

Joy erupted into action. The father saw his son in the distance and raced to meet him. His servants followed out of duty, not excitement. Upon seeing the younger son, they might have expected the father to be stoic and stern. Instead, he was kind and compassionate. If they wanted to see a fight, they had come to the wrong place.

Tachu! Tachu! Quickly! Quickly! The pending celebration of the Prodigal's return wasn't scheduled for a week from Thursday; it was to be held immediately. The father wasted no time asking, "What took you so long?" Instead, he ordered a banquet in his son's honor.

"As the father gave his orders, it became clear that he was going to hold a banquet for this son who had dishonored him so badly. He was planning to treat him the way someone might treat an honored dignitary—with gifts, a full celebration, and the ceremonial bestowal of high privileges."

1. What does the term *prodigal* mean?

    ___ Rebellious

    ___ Strong-willed

    ___ Arrogant

    ___ Extravagant

    Based on the scene now taking place, who was the Prodigal—the son or the father?

2. Read Luke 15:22–24. How do you think the Pharisees reacted to the actions of the father? Why?

"He had just sacrificed his last shred of dignity by running like a schoolboy to grant free and complete forgiveness to a son who deserved nothing more than the full weight of his father's wrath."

Rethink

The Pharisees were stunned at Jesus' description of the father's actions. The young man was stunned by the actions of his father. Everything he expected didn't happen and everything that happened wasn't expected.

The boy deserved nothing he received. As a matter of fact, he didn't even deserve the opportunity to return home. But he knew his father's love and he knew that he could never survive apart from home. Believe it or not, we're the same way!

3. The story details three gifts the father had for his son. These aren't random gifts; they had a special significance. Review the section entitled "Status" in *A Tale of Two Sons* (page 127) and list the significance of:

   a. the robe

   b. the ring

   c. the sandals

   Collectively, these items represented honor and authority. The young man was immediately restored to his rightful place in the family on the basis of what the father did, not what the son did. What does this teach about our relationship with God?

4. The father restored his son publicly. Why was this necessary? What is the significance of this action in light of your relationship with God?

"Even in our culture, it is hard to conceive of any father taking forgiveness that far. But it is yet another proof that *this* father seems not to be the least bit concerned about his own honor."

5. Read Philippians 2:6–8. Compare the attitude of the forgiving father to the attitude of Christ revealed in this passage.

6. Read Romans 4:5. What kind of people does Christ receive?

   __ Those who have kept the religious rules

   __ Those who are without hope; the filthy, and the unworthy

7. The Pharisees were disturbed that Jesus would suggest that society's outcasts could be given the privilege of a relationship with God. For the Pharisees, God was reserved for the rule-keepers and the self-righteous. Because they had been so religious, they considered themselves more worthy of God than was Jesus. What is the difference between being religious and having a relationship with God?

What is the primary goal of your life—to be religious and associate with other religious people or to have a relationship with God in which He uses you to reach those who have lost hope?

8. Review the section entitled "Privilege" in *A Tale of Two Sons* (page 132) and briefly describe the legal right known as *usufruct*. How does it apply in this story?

9. Remember that the young man had already been given his portion of the family inheritance. That is what he wasted in the distant land. All that was left belonged to the older son. Yet the older son couldn't take possession as long as the father lived. Therefore, the management of the resources remained with the father. Why didn't the father withhold material provisions from the younger son?

"In effect, what [the father] did here was lay claim to everything he had promised to the elder son, and he told the younger son, 'Use it however you like.'"

Reflect

None of this made sense, particularly in a culture where honor was so highly valued.

10. The father didn't tell the young man to clean up and then put on the robe; he put it on him as he was. What does this say about our salvation experience?

> "[The father] wanted the boy's rags covered as quickly as possible, before the Prodigal walked through the village under the disapproving gaze of so many people."

11. The robe shielded the son from the scorn his actions deserved. The ring provided access to privileges the son was not worthy of enjoying. The young man got nothing he deserved and everything he didn't deserve. Describe your spiritual life in relationship to this story.

12. The actions of the father as described by Jesus violated society's customs and common sense. How could someone so despicable be restored so ceremoniously? This is a picture of God's grace in action. Think about your life. What would you have received if you had gotten what you deserved from God?

13. The Pharisees were convinced that God's grace was earned. Jesus presented a different view of self-righteousness. Whereas the Pharisees thought self-righteousness was necessary for salvation, Jesus showed it to be a hindrance. Jesus wanted the Pharisees to see their self-righteousness as the blindfold that prevented them from seeing the truth. What are some things we do that might be considered self-righteous?

Why do you think we do these things?

React

Having ceremonially crowned his repentant son with the highest honor and privilege, the Prodigal's father was still not finished. Next, he called for the party to end all parties: "'Bring the fatted calf here and kill it, and let us eat and be merry; for this my son was dead and is alive again; he was lost and is found.' And they began to be merry" (Luke 15:23–24).

14. Everything about the father suggests that he was extremely wealthy. The use of the fattened calf was reserved for the most significant events. The homecoming of the younger son was the most significant event in the history of the family. Remember, this was a parable that taught Jesus' listeners something about God. What does this element of the story reveal about God?

His Resentment

Here is a sinner who thinks hypocrisy is as good as real righteousness.
What he looks like on the outside cloaks a seething rebellion on the inside.

— A Tale of Two Sons (p. 149)

Rewind

There are two basic varieties of sinners—the straightforward type and the secretive type. The Prodigal Son epitomizes the straightforward sinner in that he pursued self-indulgent pleasures in spite of society's disdain for such things. The older brother represents the secretive sinner—the one who often has the appearance of being religious but lives in hypocrisy.

In Jesus' parable, the Pharisees embodied this self-righteous indignation that falls into the category of secretive sin. The older brother also fits this description.

> "The elder brother turns out to be just as lost and hopelessly enslaved to sin as his brother ever was. He just won't admit that—not himself, or to anyone else."

1. Read Romans 1:28–32. Is this description fitting of the straight-forward sinner or the secretive sinner?

Rate yourself in each area from 1 to 5, with 5 being the most offensive level.

___ Unrighteousness

___ Sexual immorality

___ Wickedness

___ Covetousness

___ Maliciousness

___ Envy

___ Murder

___ Strife

___ Deceit

___ Evil-mindedness

Read the passage again. What do people who engage in these activities deserve?

2. The main lesson of the parable is embodied in the attitude of the older brother. He harbors resentment for his younger brother and a secret disrespect for his father. Read Luke 15:25–28. What is the initial response of the older brother?

___ Joy

___ Apathy

___ Anger

___ Helpfulness

"The elder son has *never* truly been devoted to his father. He is by no means symbolic of the true believer."

Rethink

The older brother had fooled a lot of people into thinking he was the "good" son. Yet, he was a hypocrite. This term carries the image of a person wearing a theatrical mask. The mask portrays a public image that is different from the real person.

3. In what ways was the sin of the older brother similar to that of the younger brother?

How was the older brother's sin different?

4. The older brother fooled the village by acting religious. Who do we try to fool in our day and time?

"Something about being shocked and outraged by the conduct of other people is just plain fun for any true Pharisee."

---

5. So far, the Pharisees had plenty of reasons to be disgusted. The behavior of the young son toward his father and his subsequent romp in the Gentile land were appalling. The young man's association with pigs was demeaning to any real person. The father's reaction to the son's return was scandalous and the banquet unnecessary. Why did the Pharisees identify with the older brother?

6. The older brother missed the events leading up to the banquet. When he returned from the field, the banquet was underway. Why are the details of the brother's return significant?

1.

2.

3.

7. Normally, the responsibility for planning a party fell to the older son. What does his lack of involvement in the party planning say about his relationship with his father?

___ His father didn't want to bother him.

___ There was a strained relationship between the older brother and the father.

___ His father knew the brother wouldn't do it right.

___ The father enjoyed planning parties.

8. The older brother did nothing to try and stop the younger brother from taking his inheritance and leaving. He did nothing to defend his father's honor. In what ways were his actions rebellious?

It is important to note that rebellion can be something we do or something we fail to do. Whereas the younger son was proactive in his rebellion, the older son was passively rebellious.

9. With the same discernment that gave the father hope for his younger son's return, he knew the heart of his older son. He knew the older son wouldn't celebrate his brother's return. What does this description say about the attitude of religious people toward repentant sinners?

> "Just as the younger son's fleeing to the far country serves to show how poorly he regarded his father, so this one's being out in the field is a fitting metaphor for where he stood in terms of his own family."

Reflect

None of this made sense, particularly in a culture where honor was so highly valued.

10. The celebration was a mystery to the older son. He could hear the music and singing, smell the roast, and hear the crowd. He could have assumed something great had happened. But he was more of a pessimist. Legalists are almost always suspicious, particularly when they encounter joyful people. How do you respond when you encounter joyful people?

> "His reaction suggests that he assumed from the get-go that whatever news had provoked such delirious joy on the part of his father was going to be something he would resent. So 'he called one of the servants and asked what these things meant' (v. 26)."

11. If the older brother's heart had been right, he would have responded differently. How do you think you would have responded in this situation?

12. The older brother demanded an explanation from one of the young servants. Read verse 27. What was the tone of the young servant's response?

It seems that even the servant boy expected the older brother to rejoice at the news of his younger brother's return. The servant's response suggested that the brother was home and that he was better than ever. How do you think the older brother felt about this news?

13. The older brother's reaction says more about his attitude toward his father than his attitude toward his brother. Why is that true?

React

Don't miss the real reason for the elder brother's intense displeasure. As we're about to see in the chapter that follows, all this pouting fury was not so much aimed at the Prodigal Son. Instead, it was focused directly against the father. This firstborn son clearly had no affection for his younger brother, but the father was the one whom he most resented.

14. The older brother was angered because the father was spending resources that eventually would be his on this party for the Prodigal Son. How do you react when your resources are used for the purpose of reaching people for God?

15. The older son cared more about himself than his father's joy. He cared about his own rights and his possessions. He cared about his bank account and his social status. Based on this description, are you more concerned about you or your Father's joy? Explain your response.

16. How do you think the Pharisees felt about the attitude of the older brother?

Read Luke 15:1–2. What was the Pharisees attitude toward Jesus?

17. The older son had no appreciation for grace or mercy. Like the Pharisees, he thought grace and mercy were earned. To offer grace and mercy without holding one to the letter of the Law was an affront to the religious structure of the society. What did the older brother and the Pharisees value most—legalism or redemption?

What do you value most?

18. The scribes and Pharisees stayed near the house of God so that people would think highly of them. They massaged their images while ignoring their faith. They practiced a dead religion—a religion that had no power in their lives and they liked it that way. Are you practicing religion or living a life of faith? What is the difference?

Pray, asking God to help you see yourself through His eyes and then commit your life to being joyful about the things that bring Him joy.

❈ T E N ❈

His True Character

*Then He forced them to acknowledge with their own lips that it is better
for an openly sinful person to repent than for someone who denies being a sinner
to shield his sin behind a facade of respectable hypocrisy.*

— A Tale of Two Sons (p. 165)

Rewind

Every time Jesus confronted the Pharisees about their hypocrisy, they departed
with a renewed commitment to prove Him wrong. They wanted to charge
Him with blasphemy, embarrass Him, or prove Him wrong.

In Matthew 21:28–32, Jesus again addressed the Pharisees regarding their
hypocrisy. He spoke to them in a parable and painted for them a striking
picture of their serious misconceptions.

"A man had two sons, and he came to the first and said,
'Son, go, work today in my vineyard.' He answered and said,
'I will not,' but afterward he regretted it and went. Then he
came to the second and said likewise. And he answered and
said, 'I go, sir,' but he did not go. Which of the two did the
will of his father?" They said to Him, "The first." Jesus said
to them, "Assuredly, I say to you that tax collectors and
harlots enter the kingdom of God before you" (vv. 28–31).

79

1. Is it better to rebel and then act in obedience or confess obedience but act in disobedience? Why?

2. In both parables, Jesus teaches that the grossest of sinners can enter the kingdom of heaven if he or she repents. Likewise, the most religious person will be excluded from heaven unless he or she repents. What, then, is most significant—a person's religious practices or a person's repentance?

Which are you most concerned about?

> "What are the characteristics of such people? Several of them are clearly evident in the Prodigal Son's elder brother as he angrily responds to his father."

Rethink

Let's pick up the scene right where we left off at the end of the previous chapter. The elder brother, returning home late, arrives to find a celebration the likes of which he has never seen. He has just learned from a servant boy that his younger brother has come home; that the father has already for-given the Prodigal and received him with joy; and that he has killed the fat-ted calf for a massive feast to celebrate the boy's redemption. As we saw in the previous chapter, the elder brother asked for and received no elabora-tion on any of those facts. He wasn't seeking further information. He had already heard enough. "He was angry and would not go in" (Luke 15:28).

3. The older brother's expression of anger was the culmination of his long-harbored resentment toward his father. What had the father done that deserved such a response?

How did the father's excitement over his younger son's return affect his feelings for his older son?

4. The Pharisees began to get the picture that the older brother in the story was representative of them. What gave them that idea?

___ The older brother's kindness

___ The older brother's hard work in the field

___ The older brother's joy

___ The older brother's refusal to go into the celebration

"Remember, what set off this string of parables in the first place was the complaint of the scribes and Pharisees that Jesus 'receives sinners and eats with them.' Everything from that statement (v. 2) until 'he . . . would not go in' (v. 28) has built relentlessly to this point, and the sinfulness of the Pharisees' attitude was about to be unmasked."

5. The remainder of Luke 15 pictures an attitude of joy. The shepherd found his sheep and the woman found her coin. The father now expresses his joy at finding his son. The only person in all three parables who is not joyful is the older son. In refusing to go in, the older son excludes himself from the joy of heaven. When it comes to dealing with God, who makes the rules?

6. The Pharisees expected the Messiah to conform to their image and to use them to save the world. Jesus' continual challenge to their authority angered them. Jesus wasn't the kind of Savior they anticipated. They were right that sinners don't deserve forgiveness and eternal life. Their mistake was in assuming they did deserve forgiveness and eternal life. Why was this a mistake?

7. Apart from God's grace, we are powerless against sin. To scorn God's grace is to condemn ourselves to a life of habitual, uncontrollable sin. We can do nothing to earn forgiveness and grace. So, how do we get forgiveness and grace?

8. Review the characteristics of the father, the older son, and the younger son. The father's love extended to both of his sons. He didn't love one more than the other. Read Luke 15:28. What did the father do when he discovered his older son was outside?

What does this say about God when we are outside His love because of sin in our lives?

9. Read Luke 15:29–30. What were the complaints of the older son? What was the tone of the conversation with his father?

"The elder son's self-assessment is one of the most telling aspects of his whole rant. Listen as he expresses the typical hyperinflated self-image of a religious hypocrite: 'I never transgressed your commandment at any time' (v. 29)."

Reflect

10. Hypocrisy feeds pride. When we see someone do something reprehensible, we often reply with self-righteous indignation more characteristic of the Pharisees than of God. Why is it so easy to be so hard on others?

"Because the hypocrite *pretends* to be good, he is under the illusion that he has actually *done* good—and therefore he thinks he *is* good."

11. When you do something wrong, how do you respond?

    __ I have a good reason.

    __ It was someone else's fault.

    __ It's not as wrong as it could have been.

    __ I have sinned against God and need forgiveness.

12. Sinful hearts have an amazing capacity for self-deception. The older son thought he had done nothing wrong and, therefore, deserved everything that had been given the younger son. What was the main attitudinal difference between the two sons?

13. The older brother was concerned only about himself. He liked it better when his brother was in the Gentile territory. What does this say about the older brother's understanding of authentic redemption?

React

Even though it appears the father knew all along that the elder son's heart was not right, such a sudden barrage of cold-hearted rebellion must have caught him a little off guard. It was a stark departure from the normal passive-aggressive style the boy had perfected.

14. Read Luke 15:31–32. What was the tone of the father's response to his older son?

15. When the son showed disrespect, the father showed love. What does this say about God?

16. Are you more patient with prodigals or hypocrites? Why?

17. Jesus' intent wasn't to prove the Pharisees wrong; it was to help them discover their need for redemption. Have you experienced this redemption? If so, explain how it happened. If not, explain why it hasn't happened,

Jesus' plea to the Pharisees is His plea to you. Will you enter into the joy that comes only from God's throne?

╣ ELEVEN ╠

The Shocking Real-Life Ending

Of all the surprising plot twists and startling details, this is the culminating surprise: Jesus marvelously shaped the point and then simply walked away without resolving the tension between the father and his firstborn.

— A Tale of Two Sons (p. 190)

React

The abrupt end to the parable leaves many wondering if there might not have been more to the story. Jesus, however, was very deliberate in His methodology. He left His hearers then and His readers now waiting for the punch line.

Even the people in the story don't know the end of the story. The father had gone outside to speak with his older son. The story ended before he returned.

> "But with all that pent-up expectation Jesus simply walked away, leaving the tale hanging, unfinished, unresolved."

1. Jesus left the father's tender appeal as the final words. He wanted the audience to meditate on it; He wants the same for you. When you consider the father's appeal to his older son, what thoughts come to mind?

How does it reflect God's character?

2. If you wrote the end of this story, what would happen?

"Don't forget that Jesus told this parable—including the abrupt ending—chiefly for the benefit of the scribes and Pharisees. It was really a story about them. The elder brother represented them."

The next response is up to the hearer—the Pharisees then, you today. We know how the Pharisees responded—they plotted and eventually killed Jesus. You have a similar choice to make.

3. Read Mark 14:1. What was the intent of the scribes and Pharisees?

If the older son in the parable followed the example of the scribes and Pharisees, what would have happened to his father?

4. What other options did the scribes and Pharisees have in response to Jesus' ministry?

> "Christ's death on the cross occurred at their urging just a few months after this encounter in Luke 15. Then they congratulated themselves on a righteous act that they were certain would preserve the honor of Israel and the true religion they believed was embodied in their beloved traditions."

5. Jesus was indeed killed, but the story didn't end there. He rose just as He said He would and He later ascended into heaven where He sits at the right hand of His Father. How does this reality affect your daily life?

6. The choice is now yours. Follow Jesus in humble obedience or reject His offer of love. No one can make the decision for you.

And it doesn't matter whether you are an open sinner like the Prodigal Son; a secret one like his elder brother; or someone with characteristics from each type. If you are someone who is still estranged from God, Christ urges you to acknowledge your guilt, admit your own spiritual poverty, embrace your heavenly Father, and be reconciled to Him.

CHAPTER 1

Read Chapter 1 of *A Tale of Two Sons* and complete the activities in Chapter 1 of the Study Guide.

Rewind

Write *prodigal* on the board and call for volunteers to suggest synonyms or definitions. List responses on the board. Point out that *prodigal living* is characterized by wasteful extravagance and wanton immorality. Call for class members to suggest some things they have done that might fall into the category of being "wastefully extravagant." This discussion should be kept lighthearted and humorous.

Call for volunteers to suggest some possible reasons Jesus told the parable of the prodigal son. Point out that it wasn't told for the purpose of improving His reputation as a great storyteller, but rather to illustrate some truths about God.

"The meaning of Scripture is not fluid. The truth of the Bible doesn't change with time or mean different things in different cultures. Whatever the text meant when it was originally written, it still means today" (p. 5). Briefly review some of the characteristics of life in the first century touching on the tension that existed between the Jewish hierarchy and Jesus.

1. Call for volunteers to share their initial understandings of the meaning of the parable of the prodigal son.

2. Read aloud Mark 12:37, highlighting the fact that Jesus spoke so that the average person could relate to His message.

Rethink

There are several parables recorded by Luke but not recorded by other biblical writers. This doesn't call into question the legitimacy of these parables because we know that Luke was intimately acquainted with Judaism and the tension between it and Jesus' ministry. Luke recorded the stories under the inspiration of the Holy Spirit. Just like the rest of the Word of God, they are vitally relevant to our lives.

3. Draw a horizontal line on the board (similar to that found on page 3 in the Study Guide) and label Jesus' baptism, temptations, final arrival in Jerusalem, His arrest, crucifixion, and resurrection. Place an X on the line just before the mark representing His final arrival in Jerusalem. Point out that this parable was told with Jesus' full understanding of His impending arrest and the role the scribes and Pharisees would play in His death.

4. Ask learners to identify some of the reasons the scribes and Pharisees opposed Jesus' ministry. Point out that the Jews anticipated a militaristic Messiah, not one who would accept sinners and Gentiles.

5, 6, 7. Call for volunteers to suggest some adjectives that describe the scribes and Pharisees. List responses on the board. If they are not suggested, add to the list *legalistic* and *hypocritical*. Take a few moments to discuss examples of how these two characteristics can manifest themselves in the lives of modern-day believers.

8. Jesus never entered into negotiations with the scribes and Pharisees; He stood His ground. Discuss some situations in which believers are tempted to negotiate with society rather than stand their ground. What are the consequences of negotiating rather than standing up for biblical truth?

9. Enlist a volunteer to read aloud Matthew 23:2–12. Each synagogue had a seat that was "Moses' seat." It was a place of authority. Of course the scribes were the designated teachers of the Law of Moses. In effect, Jesus said, "Do what they say, but don't do what they do." This was a reference to the hypocrisy of the scribes and Pharisees. They knew God's Word but had interpreted it to suit their attitudes and desires.

   The scribes and Pharisees had established a religion that was characterized by hatred and envy. Yet they tried to appear spiritual by wearing on their foreheads or arms small boxes containing portions of Scripture (phylacteries). In addition, the hems of the garments worn by religious officials were adorned with tassels that reminded the wearer of God's laws. Some zealous scribes and Pharisees enlarged their tassels so as to appear even more devoted to God. They were more concerned about appearing to be spiritual than actually being spiritual. Discuss some examples of this attitude in modern culture. What is the danger of being overly concerned with external appearances of spirituality?

Reflect

10. The primary source of disgust for the scribes and Pharisees were the gross sinners and tax collectors. The gross sinners were those who had committed a notorious offense. What might be some of those offenses in today's world? The tax collectors were despised because they were often manipulative and cruel when collecting taxes for the Roman government. Associating with either group was enough to raise the ire of the scribes and Pharisees. Jesus didn't associate with one group of outcasts; He associated with every kind of outcast. Why was this a problem for the scribes and Pharisees?

    Jesus explained His actions by telling three stories or parables. A parable is a story that has one primary point. We make a mistake to analyze every element of a parable. Doing so often interferes with our ability to grasp the real meaning.

11. Read aloud Luke 15:1–7 and discuss the relevance of the story to the culture. Point out that the presence of sheep in the area made the story familiar to all who heard it. The main point of the parable of the lost sheep is the fact that God is concerned about the salvation of the lost.

12. The parable of the lost coin was relevant because the silver coin represented a day's wages for a Roman soldier. Based on an average salary of $40,000, the lost coin represented approximately $167.00 (based on working 20 days per month). Most people would take the time to search for this amount of money because it is significant. Read aloud Luke 15:8–10. Discuss the main point of this parable—that God is concerned about the salvation of the lost.

React

13, 14. Draw on the board a horizontal line labeling the left extreme *Hesitant/Exclusive* and the right extreme *Willing/Welcoming*. Place a mark in the center of the line. To the far left write *Pharisees* and to the far right write *Jesus*. Discuss the evidence and dangers of being spiritually exclusive. Work together to create a list of ways your class and/or your church can become more inclusive in its appeal.

Read aloud Luke 5:30–32. Ask class members to quietly reflect on these verses asking themselves if they genuinely reflect Jesus' attitude or if they are more like the Pharisees in dealing with undesirable people. Brainstorm some things that can be done to reach out to those who do not know Jesus Christ as Lord and Savior.

15. Ask class members to prayerfully consider what they expect God to do in their lives through this study. Read aloud the responses to that question (found on page 8 in the Study Guide).

16. Pray, asking God to make each person in the room teachable and then willing to become the kind of person God intends. Close with prayer.

CHAPTER 2

Read chapter 2 of *A Tale of Two Sons* and complete the activities in chapter 2 of the Study Guide.

Rewind

1. Write *undesirables* on the board and call for volunteers to suggest some ways that believers might respond to people who aren't like them. List responses on the board. Discuss how God rejoices over one who is saved, and that He must be heartbroken whenever His children exclude and interfere with someone coming to embrace His love.

2. Call for volunteers to share their experiences in which they were pursued by God. Allow two or three people to share. Be prepared to share your own story if necessary.

   Discuss some of the personal challenges that must be overcome in order for us to pursue relationships with people who need to experience God's grace and love.

   Read aloud the sidebar (found on page 10): "He was a true friend of sinners—the most authentic kind of friend. He served them and reached out to them and laid hold of their lives." Discuss some of the things that we can do in order to reach out to people and lay hold of their lives for God. List responses on the board.

Rethink

3. Discuss what practical steps members can take to reach out to the spiritually needy people in their lives (such as unsaved family members, friends, neighbors, and co-workers)?

4. Ask volunteers to identify how they respond when they see someone they know ministering to an undesirable person. How would you have responded to Jesus' associating with people society despised? Discuss responses.

5. It was the sinners, not the self-proclaimed religious people, who eagerly followed Jesus. Why do you think this was so? Who today is more likely to pursue a relationship with God—people who think they have their lives in good order or people who recognize that they have spiritual needs? Why?

6. How should Jesus' example affect our ministries today? List responses on the board. Point out that Jesus concerned Himself more with the needs of people than the threats of those who were outwardly religious yet lacked love and compassion for those in need.

7. The scribes and Pharisees worked hard to convince people not to follow Jesus. Many people listened because they had been taught to respect and honor the scribes and Pharisees. To what are people listening today and what is the effect on their spiritual understanding and desires? Discuss how we should respond to those false authorities, based on 2 Corinthians 10:3–6.

8. What are some topics about which the Bible and society disagree? What are some of the ways believers respond when the Bible and society disagree? How does this compare to the opposition Jesus faced from the religious crowd?

9. Read Luke 14:26–35. Lead a brief discussion about the cost of discipleship.

In regard to this passage, the use of the word "hate" can be of concern. It is better stated as a lesser love. Jesus wanted His disciples to be so devoted to Him that any other devotion would seem like hatred in comparison. The crowd that followed Jesus was in favor of Him, but had expressed no commitment to Him. Jesus didn't change His expectations in order to get them to follow. Instead, He explained the cost of discipleship. When Jesus spoke of total commitment, He spoke of more than the abandonment of one's possessions; He required total surrender. The commitment to Jesus was without reservation.

Reflect

10. The parables in Luke 15 all make the same point. The prime targets of these parables were the hypocritical practices of the scribes and Pharisees. Toward whom would these parables be addressed in our culture and why?

Sheep are not known for being the most intelligent animals. The first mention of sheep in the Bible is in Genesis 4:2 where Abraham is identified as a keeper of sheep. The male sheep had horns that were used to make trumpets or *shophars*. Sheep came to symbolize people without leadership and unity. To what extent does our culture reflect the characteristics of sheep?

11. Read Isaiah 40:11 and discuss the image depicted in that verse as it compares to the early Christian symbol of the shepherd carrying the sheep on his shoulders.

The biblical picture shows that Jesus did all the redemptive work that was necessary. Yet many people today still believe they must do something to warrant God's grace. What are some of the things people do to attempt to earn their salvation? How should we respond to people who hold this errant viewpoint?

React

12, 13. In the parables in Luke 15, the desperate search was the result of something valuable being lost. First there was the sheep, then the coin, then a son. In all three situations, finding the lost item or person resulted in a great celebration. Based on these parables, what can we do to make God happy? How can we be instrumental in bringing lost people to salvation?

14. Make two columns on the board with the headings of Luke 15:1–7 and Luke 15:8–10. Quickly review each parable, identifying in each what was lost, who played the role of the seeker, and the reaction to the recovery of the lost item.

15. In preparation for the study of the parable of the prodigal son, refer to the matching activity on page 17 in the Study Guide. The correct responses are as follows:

A. The younger brother (The person who is lost)

B. The father (God)

C. The older brother (The Pharisees)

16. Direct students to reflect on the final activity in the Study Guide, and then lead them in a time of prayer. Call upon God to reveal Himself to you through the study of this parable. Close with prayer.

CHAPTER 3

Read chapter 3 of A *Tale of Two Sons* and complete the activities in chapter 3 of the Study Guide.

Rewind

Write *villains* and *heroes* on the board and call for volunteers to suggest some pairs of characters that fit these categories. You might use characters from the Bible or from popular stories and movies.

Ask class members to decide if the Prodigal Son should be listed as a villain or a hero. List *Prodigal Son* in the column selected by the group.

1. Discuss the use of the word *prodigal* and its meaning in today's language. Tell members that "reckless wastefulness" is the best description of *prodigal.*

2. Discuss some of the reasons people find a rebellious life so attractive. List responses on the board.

   Read aloud the sidebar (found on page 20): "The young man's request, as Jesus described it, was outrageous, impudent, and grossly dishonoring to the father." Discuss some of the reasons that the young man's request would have been so dishonoring to his father and to his family.

Rethink

Ask volunteers to identify some actions that reflect an attitude of self-centeredness. How do you respond when you see someone acting this way? How should God respond when we act this way?

Call for a volunteer to briefly explain the *law of primogeniture.* Provide any missing details. Point out that this was not a situation in which the younger son wanted the inheritance for the purpose of perpetuating the family name.

3, 4. Discuss the concept of immediate gratification, List on the board some areas of life in which people seek immediate gratification. Call for volunteers to identify areas in which they are prone to seek immediate gratification. What does our inability to patiently delay gratification say about our overall attitude toward life?

5. Read the sidebar (found on page 22): "Once disowned by a father, there was almost no way for a rebellious child to come back and regain his position in the family. If wanted back at all, he must make restitution for whatever dishonor he caused the family and for whatever possessions he might have taken when he ran away. Even then, he might expect to forfeit many of the rights that he previously enjoyed as a family member. He could certainly forget about receiving any further inheritance." Discuss the father's options in response to his son's selfish request. List the options on the board. How would you respond if someone treated you the way the son treated his father? How should God respond to us when we treat Him similarly?

6. On page 49 of A Tale of Two Sons, the young man wanted to remove himself from every obligation, to cast off all restraint, and to remove himself from his father's authority. He wanted to run. What would cause a person to run from God? Call for a volunteer to describe a time when he or she ran from God. Call attention to the motivation for returning to God. How does God respond to those who choose to run from Him?

7. Review the previously discussed actions and attitudes of the younger son and discuss the bad decisions he made. You might draw a flowchart on the board to connect it all together. Point out that everything happened as a direct consequence of that initial bad decision.

8. Discuss: What might have been the young man's reasons for wanting to get away from his family? What do the young man's actions illustrate about the heart of sinful people?

9. The actions of the Prodigal Son were sure to bring shame and embarrassment on the family. How do people today respond to family situations when there is the danger of public embarrassment?

   Read the sidebar (found on page 24): "Any self-respecting father in that culture would naturally feel he *had* to disgrace the son as publicly as possible—giving him the ceremonial slap across the face, a public denunciation, formal dismissal from the family, and possibly even a funeral." What do you think prevented the father from publicly disgracing or disowning his son?

Reflect

The granting of the inheritance by the father was enough to get the attention of the scribes and Pharisees. What is the spiritual significance of this action?

10. Write *livelihood* on the board and call for volunteers to suggest some synonyms. List responses on the board. Be sure to list *life* and *property*. Point out that the father gave more than money to the son.

11. Discuss the relationship between the father's response to his son and God's response toward us when we turn our backs on Him.

React

12. Write the following words on the board: *mercy*, *lovingkindness*, *goodwill*, and *longsuffering*. Call for volunteers to share stories regarding their experiences with God and His showing of these characteristics.

13. Discuss: Why doesn't God prevent us from rebelling against His will for our lives? What are the consequences of rebelling against God's will?

14. Briefly discuss the strengths and weaknesses of the younger son.

15. Direct students to reflect on times when they have been disobedient to God and made shameless demands of him. Lead them to ask for forgiveness and restoration. Close with prayer.

CHAPTER 4

Read chapter 4 of A *Tale of Two Sons* and complete the activities in chapter 4 of the Study Guide.

Rewind

Write *freedom* on the board and call for volunteers to suggest some ways in which people exercise their freedom. List responses on the board.

1. Call for a volunteer to read aloud Luke 15:13. Discuss the phrase "gathered all together" and point out that it means "liquidated his possessions." Call for a volunteer to share about a time when he or she wanted to run away.

2. Point out that the younger son had to accept less than market value because ownership of possessions that belonged to his father couldn't be transferred until after his father's death. The things he liquidated were virtually worthless to the person who purchased them.

   Call for volunteers to suggest some reasons the young man was so eager to get away from his family and community. What causes people to run away today? List responses on the board.

Rethink

3. Ask volunteers to share some things that people do to run away from their life situations. List responses on the board. Call attention to modern situations to which this parable speaks.

Consider adding *relationships*, *work*, *hobbies*, *sports*, and so forth to the list.

4. List on the board *family*, *God*, and *authority*. Ask volunteers to suggest some reasons people would run from these. Focus on the act of running from God. Refer to the story of Jonah if time allows. Discuss the personal consequences of running from God. What are the societal effects of a person's running from God?

5. Call attention to the chart on page 31 in the Study Guide and discuss the severity of the younger brother's materialism, greed, and foolishness. Then direct students to evaluate their lives using the same chart. Point out that prodigal living produces extremes in these three areas.

6. Discuss the reasons the scribes and Pharisees would demonize the young man for running to a Gentile land. Point out that the Jewish hierarchy held in contempt anyone who was not a Jew.

7. To the scribes and Pharisees, the younger son was despicable. He turned his back on everything that was the norm—his faith, his family, and his culture. What are the characteristics of the despicable people in our culture and how do we usually respond to them?

8. Consider the older brother. Why didn't he step in and correct the younger brother? What do his actions say about his attitude toward his faith, his family, and his culture? Point out that there are two kinds of sin—sins of commission and sins of omission. Doing nothing often is as sinful as doing the wrong thing.

9. Read the sidebar (found on page 33): "Although the father was a loving, generous, kindly man who provided abundant gifts for

his two sons, both of his sons cared more for the father's wealth than they did for the father himself." Point out that in this question in the Study Guide that the correct answer is: "He didn't really love his father either."

What are things we care more for than care for God? List responses on the board. Why are these things so important?

Reflect

10. The younger son headed for Gentile land with the sole purpose of having fun. He was more concerned about having fun than anything else. How did this desire affect his relationship with his family, his community, and God? Where do we run to escape today's realities? What do we hope to accomplish by running? How are we affected in these areas (family, community, and God) when our primary pursuit is having fun?

11. Read aloud Galatians 6:7–8. How does this passage respond to our desire for pleasure above responsibility? Encourage students to commit this passage to memory.

React

Sin never delivers what it promises. Make two columns on the board and head the first column *promises* and the second column *delivers*. Call for volunteers to suggest some things that sin promises. List those ideas in the first column, then list the opposite idea in the second column.

12. Call for volunteers to read aloud the following passages: Romans 6:23, Romans 8:13, and James 1:15. Point out each passage's words regarding sin.

13, 14. Ask volunteers to identify the connection between self-gratification and godly peace. Point out that the two are at opposite ends of the spectrum. We choose to pursue one or the other.

Use a rubber band to illustrate the point. Hold the rubber band with one hand representing God and the other hand representing self-gratification. Begin to stretch the rubber band calling attention to the tension being generated. Tension in our lives often is the result of our pursuit of self-gratification rather than God.

15, 16, 17. Read the description of the European famine on page 66 in *A Tale of Two Sons*. Discuss the severity of the famine and how terrible it must be to be that hungry. This was the end result of the young man's pursuit of his own desires. What should we say to someone we know who has similar pursuits? Ask the group to consider the ways in which they have been prodigals and have run from God. Close with prayer, asking God to restore members into right relationships with him.

CHAPTER 5

Read chapter 5 of *A Tale of Two Sons* and complete the activities in chapter 5 of the Study Guide.

Rewind

Write *self-indulgence* on the board and call for volunteers to suggest some things we do that might seem to fit the meaning of this term. List responses on the board.

1, 2. Call for a volunteer to read aloud Luke 15:17. Recap the early part of the Prodigal's life, reminding the class that the young man had squandered the cash value he received for his inheritance. Ask class members to suggest some thoughts that might have been running through the young man's mind.

Had the young man known the end result of his decision to leave his father's home, he probably wouldn't have left. Why do you think we don't take the time to consider the possible consequences of our decisions before we make the decisions? How would the practice of considering the consequences affect our daily decisions?

Review Luke 15:17, calling attention to the phrase "when he came to himself." Call for volunteers with other translations to read aloud the verse. Ask class members to discuss the meaning of the term. Point out that the correct response in the Study Guide is: "When he thought through his situation from a truthful perspective."

Rethink

3. Read aloud Luke 15:13–16 and call for volunteers to share how they think they would have responded to this situation.

4. List on the board *pride* and *stubbornness*. Ask volunteers to identify some ways they are affected by these two tendencies.

5. Discuss the difference between looking for a job and becoming a persistent beggar. Explain that the job of feeding pigs was the most demeaning job to be had in this time in history. Out of desperation, the young man took the job. What might be the most demeaning job in your community and what do you think motivates people to take those jobs?

6. Explain the reasons the scribes and Pharisees would have been disgusted with the young man and his job. The Prodigal had abandoned his family, sold his inheritance, moved to a foreign land, lived an immoral life, and associated with pigs. On a scale of one to ten, the scribes and Pharisees were at a one in their compassion for the young man!

7, 8. The young man was desperate. His condition affected his judgment. In what ways have you been desperate and how did it affect your judgment? What did that experience teach you about God?

9. Discuss the carob pods and the fact that these were only usable as an emergency food supply for livestock. They represented hope in the midst of a famine. To what or to whom do we turn when our circumstances get difficult?

Read the sidebar (found on page 41): "In the Pharisees' estimation, [the Prodigal] had essentially *become* one of the pigs. The only way he could get any lower was to be cast into the pit of hell—which, as far as the Pharisees were concerned, was practically unavoidable for him now and a punishment well deserved." What are some of our reasons for declaring people unworthy of anything except hell? What does this attitude say about our understanding of grace?

Reflect

10. Draw a horizontal line on the board. Label the left end *contempt* and the right end *compassion*. When you see someone who has made choices on par with those made by the Prodigal, what is your attitude? Be willing to share your own attitude and how God has worked to change it. Point out that God's attitude is one of compassion. Call for volunteers to share ideas regarding the reasons we so easily embrace attitudes that are inconsistent with God's attitudes.

11, 12. Arrange the class in smaller groups and instruct each group to spend a few minutes discussing their present relationships with God in terms of . . .

   a. The quality and quantity of the time spent in daily devotion to Him.

b. Their desire to please God with every aspect of their lives.

c. Their desire to give God their best.

After a few moments, call for groups to share what they learned in this exercise. Point out that this should help us discover our need for improvement in our relationships with God.

React

13. Read aloud Ephesians 2:12. The Gentiles were alienated for two reasons: social and spiritual. On the social front, the Gentiles and Jews had been at odds for a long time. To the Jews, the Gentiles were outcasts. From the spiritual perspective, the Gentiles had no access to God. Is it more devastating to be alienated socially or spiritually? Why?

14, 15. Read aloud Romans 8:7–8. Point out that enmity against God means an inner hostility toward God. It is more than simply acting in disobedience. The desire to pursue self-gratification rather than pursuing God's goodness is evidence of a person's enmity against God.

16, 17. Write on the board: *spiritual bankruptcy, emptiness, destruction, destitution,* and *loneliness.* Point out that these are the consequences of living life according to the world's ways. Call for volunteers to suggest some opposites for these terms. Point out that these are the by-products of living according to God's ways. Close with prayer.

CHAPTER 6

Read chapter 6 of A *Tale of Two Sons* and complete the activities in chapter 6 of the Study Guide.

Rewind

Write *righteousness* on the board and call for volunteers to suggest meanings for the term. List responses on the board. Discuss some things people do in pursuit of righteousness.

1. Discuss some of the obstacles people face in their desire for repentance. Be sure to mention pride and self-righteousness as possible obstacles.

2. Read aloud Luke 15:17–19. List some of the ways the young man sinned. He sinned by turning his back on his father, his family responsibilities, his faith, and his nation. He sinned by living an immoral life and squandering the money he had. He sinned by believing that he could solve the problem on his own. In what ways are these attitudes prevalent in our lives today?

Rethink

3. Why do you think it is so hard for us to make an honest evaluation of our lives?

4. Use the activity to help you understand how you prioritize sources of help. Discuss the reasons people delay seeking God. Be willing to share a personal word regarding your delaying your dependence on God.

5. If the Prodigal returned home, what might have been his father's reaction? List responses on the board.

6. Read aloud Romans 6:16. New believers have an innate desire to know and obey God's Word (see 1 Peter 2:2). If the innate desire for God's Word is natural for believers, what might someone conclude about your salvation based on your desire for God's Word?

Arrange the class in small groups and instruct each group to list some of God's characteristics. After a few moments, call for the groups to add their characteristics to a list on the board. Point out that when we think of God, these are the characteristics we should remember.

7. The young man's situation was critical. If he kept doing what he was doing, he would keep receiving what he was receiving—and death was in the immediate future. Point out that the young man had to come to grips with his needs and wants. How do we determine needs and wants? Have you ever considered something a need that really was a want? Why did you do that?

8. True repentance begins with the accurate assessment of one's condition. Discuss the Prodigal's condition from the perspective of God's Word. Why do you think it is so hard for people to see themselves as they really are?

9. Rethink the Prodigal Son's descent down the social ladder. He began as a "spoiled child" with everything he needed and wanted. His greed got the best of him and he left his family, faith, and culture. He squandered his resources in immoral activities, lost his friends, and ended up as a hired hand on a pig farm. Discuss the transition in the young man's attitude toward his father's servants before he left home and now that he was planning a return home. What caused the change in attitude?

Reflect

10. What characteristics of God do you remember most often? List responses on the board.

Call attention to the sidebar (found on page 15): "The Greek word for "repentance" throughout the New Testament is *metanoia*, and its literal meaning speaks of a change of mind—a reversal in one's thinking." Make sure that the class members understand the concept of biblical repentance.

11. Read aloud Ezekiel 11:19–20. Ezekiel's viewpoint of repentance incorporated a new way of seeing every aspect of life. Why is it so necessary to recast your thinking as a part of repentance? Point out this necessity of changing our thinking because God's ways are not man's ways. Once we accept Jesus Christ as our Savior, we must begin to all of see life from God's perspective.

12. Discuss the role of brokenness in the act of repentance.

React

13. Point out the difference between remorse and repentance. Remorse (or regret) is feeling bad because you got caught. Repentance is the result of the realization that you have hurt someone you love—God.

14. Write *repentance* on the board and then write *mercy*. Draw a line connecting repentance to mercy while pointing out that repentance leads us to seek mercy. Remorse leads us to seek excuses.

15. Read aloud Ezra 9:6 and Luke 9:23. Ezra realized the enormous size of his sin and his need for God to wipe it away. Jesus suggested that true repentance calls for one to daily follow Christ. Why is it so hard for people to actually repent?

16. Read aloud Luke 15:20. The Prodigal realized that he needed to confess to the one he had wronged—his father. When we seek repentance, we need to confess to the One we wronged—God.

17. The young man headed home a changed person. His arrogance was replaced by humility. His self-sufficiency was replaced by a

realization of his need for mercy. Ask volunteers to share how their repentance affected their lives. Close with prayer.

CHAPTER 7

Read chapter 7 of A *Tale of Two Sons* and complete the activities in chapter 7 of the Study Guide.

Rewind

1. Write *forgiveness* on the board and call for volunteers to suggest meanings for the term. List responses on the board. Discuss some things people do that result in a need for forgiveness.

2. The Pharisees opposed instant forgiveness in favor of a progressive forgiveness in which the person would earn forgiveness over time. When it comes to forgiveness, in what ways are we like the Pharisees?

Rethink

3. Call for volunteers to suggest some situations in which forgiveness might be in order. List responses on the board. In which of those situations would it be very hard to forgive someone else? In which would it be difficult to forget the offense and fully restore the relationship? Which of those situations would require a lot of time to heal? What does this highlight about the quickness and completeness of God's forgiveness?

   Point out that the magnificent truth is that we could never earn God's forgiveness, as the Pharisees believed. When we come to Him in heartfelt repentance, having placed our faith fully in the death of Christ, we are instantly and totally forgiven.

   Read aloud Psalm 103:12. God puts our sins away as far as the east is from the west. If you consider a globe, and begin moving around the globe to the east, you never get to the point where the direction you are moving changes and becomes the west. Therefore, the east and the west are not connected. But if you move north on the globe, once you reach the North Pole, your direction changes and you begin moving south. Therefore, the north and south are connected.

4. Call for volunteers to suggest how the father might have responded to his son if the father had followed the philosophy of the Pharisees. Read the sidebar (found on page 57): "So what happened next was a seismic jolt to the Pharisees' worldview. Their eyes would roll and their heads would shake with shock and outrage at the reception the father gave the Prodigal Son." Why did the father's response flabbergast the Pharisees?

5. Make two columns on the board. Label the first column *The father's resources*. (Note that *father* should be lowercase.) Call for volunteers to suggest some of the resources the young man's father had. List responses in the first column and discuss why the young man needed these resources. Then label the second column *The Father's resources*. (*Father* should be uppercase.) List God's resources and discuss why we need His resources.

6. Read aloud Luke 15:18–19. Discuss the young man's expectations regarding the reception he would receive upon his return home. Why did he believe he was deserving of this kind of reception?

7. The young man deserved the harshest treatment because he had been so disrespectful to his father. In what ways are we like the young man in our attitudes and actions toward God? What do we deserve in return? It is God's love and His grace that allows Him to be forgiving and loving. God loves us because of who He is; not because of who we are.

8. The terms of the son's return were totally dependent on the will of the father. The son could do nothing except accept the terms or return to the Gentile pig farm. When we come to God, we come to God on His terms. What are some things people do in an effort to set the terms of their salvation?

9. Read aloud Genesis 50:15–21. Point out that the story of Joseph's forgiveness of his brothers is an example of God's mercy on those who deserve strict judgment. It is important, however, to point out that sin has consequences. Being forgiven erases the guilt, but we often must live with the natural consequences in this life. If possible, relate a personal story regarding the consequences of something you did. It is critical that we don't suggest that believers can do whatever they want and not be held accountable by God.

Reflect

10. Read aloud Luke 15:20. The father anxiously anticipated his son's return. He scanned the horizon from a high place on his property. His love for his son would not let him lose hope. What does this image say about God?

    Read the sidebar (found on page 59): "Obviously, the heartache had not yet worn off, because the father was still watching. And he kept watching daily, heartbroken but hopeful, privately bearing the unspeakable pain of suffering love for his son." The heartbroken father longed for his son to return to the place he belonged. There are many people who have abandoned their relationships with God for a variety of reasons. What is God's attitude toward them?

11. Because the father anticipated his son's return, he had rehearsed it over and over in his mind. The villagers had heard about the rebellion of the young man. How might have the villagers treated

the young man? When it comes to the salvation of other people, in what ways are we like the villagers?

12. In Romans 8:30 Paul used the past tense to describe a future event. *Predestined* means "to point out, appoint, or determine beforehand." *Called* implies that salvation is by God's prerogative. *Justified* means "to be declared righteous." Righteousness isn't possible except by the declaration of God. *Glorified* refers to the ultimate Christlikeness that is promised to all believers.

React

13. When the father saw his son in the distance, he ran to him. Running signifies the sheer joy of the father. This was the moment he had been anticipating. He wanted to get to his son before anyone sent him away. What does this teach us about God?

14. Write on the board: *The son deserved* . . . and *The father gave*. . . . List some of the things the son deserved and what the father gave. The father gave love, acceptance, forgiveness, and so forth. What does this teach about God?

15. The son had prepared his plea but the father paid no attention. The young man's actions revealed the condition of his heart. What he did was far more significant than what he said. The condition of our hearts is affected by our relationship to God. List some things believers can do to deepen their relationships with God.

16. Review the section in *A Tale of Two Sons* (pages 120–123) regarding the substitutionary atonement that is pictured in the Old Testament sacrificial system and in the New Testament death of Jesus Christ. Share your salvation experience and call for others to share theirs. Pray, asking God to stir the hearts of those who

have yet to seek salvation. Be prepared to speak with anyone who might need to discuss his or her salvation. Close with prayer.

CHAPTER 8

Read chapter 8 of A *Tale of Two Sons* and complete the activities in chapter 8 of the Study Guide.

Rewind

1. Write *joy* on the board and call for volunteers to suggest some things that bring about joy. Discuss the differences between joy and happiness. Point out that joy is rooted in one's relationship with God and happiness is a response to one's circumstances in life. Remind the class that *prodigal* means extravagant. As the scene shifts, the extravagant character is no longer the son; it is the father. Discuss the significance of this act in light of our understanding of God.

2. Read aloud Luke 15:22–24. Discuss the expectations of the Pharisees regarding the father's reaction to the son. They would have expected a harsh reaction because of the son's disrespectful behavior.

Rethink

3. Refer to the section in A *Tale of Two Sons* entitled "Reinstating His Son's Status" (page 127) for the discussion of the significance of the robe, the ring, and the sandals. Collectively, the father's awarding of these items to the son represented his restoration to a position of power and authority in the family and in the community.

4. The public restoration signified to the village that the young man had been forgiven and restored. Any scorn they had for him had

to be replaced with the respect the father reestablished. What is the connection of this event to the salvation experience?

5. Read aloud Philippians 2:6–8. List the characteristics of Christ as revealed in this passage. Compare this list to the characteristics of the father as revealed in this portion of the parable. In what ways is the father like Christ?

6. Call for a volunteer to read aloud Romans 4:5. Point out that Christ receives those who are without hope—the filthy and the unworthy—people just like the Prodigal Son and just like us!

7. Write on the board: *religion* and *relationship*. Discuss the differences between being religious and having an authentic relationship with God. Why do so many people seek to do religious things rather than establish a relationship with God? Which is easier to do?

8. Discuss the concept of *usufruct* and its relevance to this story. For a better understanding, see the section in *A Tale of Two Sons* entitled "Restoring His Son's Privilege."

9. The young man had squandered his inheritance. There was nothing left for him. Yet the father gave him access to everything he had. Why did the father do this? What does it teach us about God?

Reflect

10, 11. Some people say they can't come to God until they get their lives cleaned up. How does the image of the father placing the robe on his filthy son respond to that rationale?

12. It is a good thing that God doesn't give us what we deserve. If God gave us what we deserve, what would we receive? List responses on the board. Why doesn't God give us what we deserve? Point out that God's love and grace determines His response to us.

13. Draw a circle in the middle of the board and write in it self-righteousness. Draw an arrow from the left and label it *Pharisees*. Discuss how the Pharisees viewed self-righteousness as being necessary for a right relationship with God. Then draw an arrow from the right pointing at the circle and label it *Jesus*. Discuss how Jesus saw self-righteousness as an obstacle to a right relationship with God. Ask the class to determine which view of self-righteousness is most appropriate today and why.

React

14. Call for volunteers to identify some of the most significant family events in their lives. Ask them to identify some of the preparations and activities associated with the events. Call attention to the banquet preparations ordered by the father. Based on his actions, this was the most significant event in the family's history. What does this teach us about God's attitude toward a repentant sinner?

    The celebration was for the benefit of the father. The cause of the celebration was the son's return. The father, however, wanted to share his joy with the community. Authentic joy can't be contained. What are those things that bring joy into your life? For whom are you praying to experience the ultimate joy of salvation? List first names on the board.

    Read aloud Luke 15:7. Repentance ignites a celebration in heaven. How should we respond to a person's repentance?

    What are those things that rob believers of their joy? What can we do to reclaim the joy of our salvation? List responses on the board.

CHAPTER 9

Read chapter 9 of *A Tale of Two Sons* and complete the activities in chapter 9 of the Study Guide.

Rewind

Write *sin* on the board and call for volunteers to identify the two types of sinners detailed in chapter 9. The two types are straightforward and secretive. Write those two terms on the board and then write *Prodigal Son* above *straightforward* and *Older Son* over *secretive*.

1. Read aloud Romans 1:28–32. This is a description of the straightforward sinner or the Prodigal. Review the passage calling attention to the examples of each attitude or action. This is the way many unrepentant people live their lives today. According to the Bible, such people are deserving of death.

2. Read aloud Matthew 15:25–28. The brother's initial response to the apparent celebration was anger. What does his anger say about the condition of his heart?

Rethink

3, 4. The older brother's sin was similar to that of the younger brother in that he showed a total lack of respect for his father and lived a very self-centered life. It was different in that he was secretive about his sin. He played the role of a religious person very well. Why is it so easy to play the role of a religious person? Why is it so attractive?

5. Why did the Pharisees relate to the older brother? Why would he initially become the apparent hero of the story?

6. The older brother's return from the field revealed that he had travelled a long distance, he wasn't very close to his father, and he would be more of a hindrance than a help. When it comes to God's work, what do we do that parallels us to the older brother?

7. The older son's lack of involvement in the party planning revealed that there was a strained relationship between him and his father. What causes a strained relationship between us and God?

8. Write on the board: *proactive* and *passive*. Discuss these two types of sin. Which is the most common category of sin for us? Why is this a problem? What can we do to keep from sinning in either of these ways?

9. The father knew his sons. He knew the younger one would return and the older one wouldn't be happy. The older son represents religious people. Why would a religious person not celebrate the redemption of another person?

Reflect

10. Legalists are almost always suspicious, particularly when they encounter joyful people. How do you respond when you encounter joyful people? Why do we allow our faith to become so lifeless?

11. How do you think you would have responded had you been the older brother? Why would you have responded that way?

12. Even the young servant expected the son to be delighted at his brother's return. It seems the servant had more respect for the father than did the son. In the image of the redemptive event, the older brother was cold water on the fire. In what ways do we throw cold water on others' spiritual fires?

13. The older brother's anger shows his true feelings about his father. He despised everything about him, including the fact that he was still alive. What caused this to happen in this young man's life? How does this attitude creep into our lives?

React

14. Consider how your church invests resources to reach unsaved people. Why would some people be upset about this effort? With whom in the parable are people like this associated?

15. Write on the board: *rights, possessions, bank account,* and *social status.* On the other side of the board write *God's joy.* Explain that your life is focused on one or the other, but it can't be focused on both.

16. Read aloud Luke 15:1–2. What was the Pharisees' attitude toward Jesus? Why did they have this attitude?

17. The older son valued legalism over redemption. How can we keep from adopting this way of thinking?

    The scribes and Pharisees cared more about what people thought of them than they did about having a right relationship with God. What is most important to you? Are you more concerned about appearing religious or living a dynamic life of faith? Close with prayer.

CHAPTER 10

Read chapter 10 of A *Tale of Two Sons* and complete the activities in chapter 10 of the Study Guide.

Rewind

1. Write *rebel* and *obedience* on the board. Is it better to rebel and then act in obedience or confess obedience but act in disobedience? Discuss the relevance of each to the parable of the prodigal son.

2. Call for a volunteer to read aloud Matthew 21:28–32. Compare this parable to the parable of the prodigal son. Point out the similarities. In both parables, the religious people are painted in opposition to the repentant person. Is this still the way it is today? How so?

Rethink

3. What had the father done that deserved the older son's anger? Point out that the father's excitement about his younger son had no bearing on the way he felt about his older son. He would have rejoiced at his older son's redemption in the same way he rejoiced for the younger son.

4. The older brother's refusal to go into the celebration was representative of the Pharisees in that they refused to associate with Jesus because He associated with sinners.

5. Joy is the theme of the redemptive act. Heaven rejoices when a lost sinner is found. The Pharisees wanted to define how people interact with God. We must understand that God makes the rules!

6. The Pharisees assumed they deserved forgiveness and eternal life because they had done the right things. What made this a mistake? Point out that we are restored to a right relationship with God based on faith in Christ, not on works.

7. The only way to defeat sin is in God's power. To scorn grace is to submit to sin's power in our lives. Forgiveness and grace are God's offer and there is nothing we can do to deserve them.

8. Read aloud Luke 15:28. What does the father's response to the older son teach us about God? When we are outside of God's love, He pleads with us to repent. Why do some people resist His offer of forgiveness?

9. Read aloud Luke 15:29–30. The older son complained about the fact that he had done so much and deserved more than the younger son. How is this attitude evidenced in our spiritual lives?

Reflect

10. Write on the board: *Hypocrisy feeds pride*. Call for volunteers to react to the statement. Refer to the parable, citing the hypocrisy of the older brother and the pride with which he approached his father. When have you acted this way toward God?

11. Call attention to the activity (on page 84) in the Study Guide. When you do something wrong, how do you respond? Discuss responses. Why is it so easy to do everything except turn to God?

12. What was the attitudinal difference between the younger son and the older son? The younger son knew he was wrong and humbly approached his father. The older son was arrogant and more focused on what his brother had done wrong. What happens to us when we pay more attention to the sins of others than to our own sins?

13. The older brother's reaction points to the fact that he believed there was limited room in his father's circle of love. He saw it as

a competition. He didn't understand that the father's love was unlimited. This reflects the way the Pharisees viewed the kingdom of God.

React

16. Read aloud Luke 15:31–32. The father's response was compassionate and loving. What does this teach us about God's attitude toward us even when we have disappointed Him?

15. The son's disrespect was countered with the father's pleading. What does that teach us about the character of God and the nature of the gospel?

16. Write *prodigals* and *hypocrites* on the board. With which group are you most impatient? Why?

17. Call for volunteers to share their testimonies. Be prepared to speak with anyone who is uncertain about his or her salvation status. Close with prayer.

CHAPTER 11

Read chapter 11 of *A Tale of Two Sons* and complete the activities in chapter 11 of the Study Guide. Use the questions in the Study Guide to lead a brief summary of the lesson.

React

This session is all about leading people to the point of confessing their faith in Jesus Christ. It is a time for quiet reflection and prayer. As you lead this session, be mindful of those who might need to repent and turn in faith to the Lord. If you are uncertain about this responsibility, enlist a church leader or someone else to assist.

ABOUT THE AUTHOR

John MacArthur, the author of numerous best-selling books that have touched millions of lives, is pastor-teacher of Grace Community Church in Sun Valley, California, and president of The Master's College and Seminary. He is also president of Grace to You, the ministry that produces the internationally syndicated radio program Grace to You and a host of print, audio, and Internet resources. He authored the notes in the Gold Medallion Award-winning *The MacArthur Study Bible*. For more information, contact Grace to You at 1-800-55-GRACE.